GREAN
LIGHT GO

TO MEDITATION &
MANIFESTING MILLIONS

By Tangela Huggins

Grean Light Go to Meditation & Manifesting Millions
Copyright 2023 Tangela Huggins

Illustrations by Carmen Pritson

ISBN: 979-8-9884104-4-7

Reorder at www.TangelaHuggins.com
Special discounts are available on bulk quantity purchases by book clubs, associations and special interest groups.

DEDICATION

To my dearest children Jamael, Tislum, Oluwafemi, Khalil, Antonio, Raricus and Tavian.

This book is dedicated to you, my reason and motivation for writing it. As your parent, I have always strived to provide you with the best opportunities and experiences in life. Writing this book is just one way that I hope to continue doing so.

Through this book, I hope to inspire you and others to pursue your passions and dreams, just as I have pursued mine. I want you to know that anything is possible if you work hard and believe in yourself.

Thank you for being my constant source of love and inspiration. You are the reason why I wake up every day with a renewed sense of purpose and drive.

With all my love, Mom

CONTENTS

INTRODUCTION: MANIFESTING MILLIONS 1

CHAPTER ONE: GRAVITATE YOUR GENIUS 3

CHAPTER TWO: REMOVE AND REPLENISH............................ 9

CHAPTER THREE: ENGRAVE A SOLID MINDSET..................... 13

CHAPTER FOUR: ACTION AND ACCOUNTABILITY 17

CHAPTER FIVE: NON-NEGOTIABLE 19

CHAPTER SIX: LIGHT INTO ENERGY................................... 24

CHAPTER SEVEN: GO TO THE CYCLE OF GROWTH 27

JOURNAL QUESTIONS... 31

GREAN LIGHT GO TO 31 DAYS OF MEDITATION JOURNAL....... 35

INTRODUCTION

MANIFESTING MILLIONS

Once, there was a young man named Jamael who had a genius mind for business. He dreamed of manifesting millions and living a life of abundance and luxury. However, he knew that just dreaming simply wasn't enough—he needed to take action and hold himself accountable too.

And so, Jamael began engraving a solid mindset into his daily routine. He read books on personal development, listened to motivational speakers, and practiced daily affirmations to remind himself of his goals. He also made a non-negotiable agreement with himself to remove negativity and replenish his energy with positivity and gratitude.

As Jamael went through the cycle of growth, he encountered many obstacles and setbacks. Some of his business ventures failed, and he faced rejection and criticism from friends and family. But still, he refused to give up and always reminded himself to trust the process.

With each failure, Jamael learned valuable lessons and adjusted his approach. He persevered through the tough times and celebrated his successes with gratitude and light. And slowly but surely, his hard work started to pay off.

Years later, Jamael had manifested millions in his bank account and had lived a life of abundance and fulfillment. But even with all his success, he knew his journey wasn't over yet. He continued to engrave a solid mindset, take action and hold himself accountable, and go through the cycle of growth.

For Jamael, manifesting millions wasn't just about the money - it was about becoming the best version of himself and living a purposeful life. And through his commitment to growth and self-improvement, he achieved all he had dreamed of and much more.

Through his failures, Jamael learned valuable lessons about what works and what doesn't work. He adjusted his approach by trying new things and taking different actions to achieve his goals. He also continued to educate himself and seek advice from others who had experienced success in similar areas. Overall, Jamael never gave up and remained determined to reach his goals, no matter how many times he failed along the way.

CHAPTER ONE

GRAVITATE YOUR GENIUS

Gravitate Your Genius is a story about mental motivation and transformation. Tangelina, the main character, had always believed she was not capable of achieving the greatness she saw in others. She lacked self-confidence and motivation, which made it difficult for her to achieve her goals.

One day, Tangelina stumbled upon a motivational speaker who spoke about Gravitate Your Genius—a process of discovering your inner potential and transforming your mindset to unlock your full potential. Intrigued, Tangelina decided to embark on this journey of self-discovery.

Through Gravitate Your Genius, Tangelina learned how to focus her mind on positive thoughts and reprogrammed her beliefs about what she was capable of achieving. Over time, Tangelina's mindset shifted, and she began to believe in herself and trust in her abilities.

As she continued on her journey, Tangelina discovered that mental transformation did not happen overnight. It took discipline, hard work, and constant self-reflection to continually improve her mindset. But, as she persisted through the challenges, Tangelina began to see drastic changes in her life and career.

The key takeaway from Tangelina's story is that anyone can transform their mindset and achieve their dreams. By consciously choosing positive thoughts and focusing on mental motivation, we can all unlock our inner potential and become the best version of ourselves.

There are several steps to the Gravitate Your Genius process:

1. **Self-Reflection:** This involves taking a deep look at your current mindset and beliefs in order to identify any negative thought patterns and determine your strengths and weaknesses.
2. **Goal Setting:** Once you have a better understanding of yourself, you can set specific, achievable goals that align with your values and aspirations.
3. **Mindset Shift:** Through daily affirmations, visualization, and positive self-talk, you can begin to shift your mindset towards more positive, empowering beliefs.
4. **Action Plan:** With your goals and mindset in place, it's time to create an action plan that outlines specific steps you will take to achieve your goals.
5. **Accountability:** Finally, it's important to hold yourself accountable for your progress and seek support from others who can help keep you motivated and on track.

These steps are not necessarily linear for every person and may need to be revisited as you continue on your journey of personal development.

There are a few ways to identify negative thought patterns during self-reflection:

1. **Pay attention to your inner dialogue:** What do you tell yourself on a regular basis? Are your thoughts generally positive or negative?
2. **Look for patterns in your behavior:** Do you tend to avoid certain situations or people because of negative thoughts or fears?
3. **Consider feedback from others:** Have friends or family members expressed concern about your attitude or behavior?
4. **Practice journaling:** Writing down your thoughts and feelings can help you identify patterns and triggers for negative thinking.

By becoming more aware of your negative thought patterns, you can take steps to challenge those thoughts and replace them with more positive, empowering beliefs.

There are a few effective strategies you can use to challenge negative thought patterns and replace them with positive ones:

1. **Practice self-compassion:** Be kind to yourself and take a non-judgmental approach to your thoughts and feelings.
2. **Use positive affirmations:** Repeat

positive statements to yourself, such as "I am worthy and capable" or "I choose to focus on the good in my life."

3. **Reframe negative thoughts:** Instead of getting stuck in negative thinking patterns, try to reframe your thoughts in a more positive light. For example, if you find yourself thinking "I'm not good enough," try reframing it to "I may not be perfect, but I am doing my best."

4. **Find evidence to support positive beliefs:** Look for examples in your life that support positive beliefs about yourself, such as times when you succeeded at something or received compliments from others.

5. **Practice gratitude:** Focus on things in your life for which you are grateful, and use this perspective to counteract negative thinking.

Positive affirmations can be a powerful tool in replacing negative thoughts with positive ones. They can help boost self-confidence and promote a more positive outlook on life. However, it's important to use them consistently and genuinely in order for them to be effective.

Research has shown that positive affirmations can activate certain areas of the brain which are associated with reward, motivation, and self-regulation. When we repeat positive statements to ourselves, we can train our brains to focus on the good in our lives, rather than dwelling on negative thoughts or experiences. Over time, this can lead to a more optimistic and resilient mindset, which can have a positive impact on our overall well-being. Additionally, using positive affirmations can help reduce stress and anxiety, boost self-esteem, and improve our relationships with others.

There are many different types of positive affirmations that can be effective, depending on the individual and their specific goals. Some examples include affirmations about self-love, confidence, success, and abundance. It's important to choose affirmations that resonate with you personally and feel authentic. Additionally, it can be helpful to use specific and detailed language, focus on the present moment, and avoid using negative language or statements. Consistency and repetition are also key factors in making positive affirmations work for you.

Here are a few examples:

- Instead of saying "I am successful," you could say "I am a successful business owner who provides value to my clients every day."
- Instead of saying "I love myself," you could say "I love and accept myself exactly as I am, flaws and all."
- Instead of saying "I am confident," you could say "I am confident in my ability to speak up in meetings and share my ideas with others."

Adding specific details to your affirmations can help make them more concrete and tangible and, therefore, more believable and effective.

Visualization techniques can be a powerful way to enhance the effectiveness of affirmations. When you visualize yourself experiencing or achieving what you're affirming, it can help to reinforce the positive message and make it feel more real. For example, if your affirmation is "I am successful in my career," you could visualize yourself receiving a promotion or award at work or successfully completing a challenging project. This kind of mental rehearsal can help to build confidence, motivation, and a sense of possibility.

There are many different visualization exercises that can be effective, depending on your specific goals and preferences. One common technique is guided visualizations, where you listen to a recorded audio or read a script that guides you through a specific visualization experience. Another technique is to create a vision board, which is a collection of images and words that represent your goals and aspirations. You can also simply imagine yourself in the situation you're affirming, using all of your senses to make the experience as vivid and real as possible. The key is to find a technique that works for you and to practice it consistently and genuinely.

CHAPTER TWO

REMOVE AND REPLENISH

There once was a busy executive named Tislum who struggled with time management. She always felt like there were never enough hours in the day to get everything done, and her stress levels were through the roof.

One day, Tislum attended a time management seminar where she learned about the concept of "remove and replenish." The idea was to identify tasks or activities that drained her time or energy and replace them with ones that were more productive or fulfilling.

Tislum decided to put this into practice by first identifying the time wasters in her day—scrolling through social media during breaks, checking emails constantly, and attending unnecessary meetings. She then removed these time wasters from her routine and replaced them with activities to help replenish her energy and focus, such as going for a quick walk outside or reading a few pages of a book.

At first, Tislum found it challenging to break her old habits, but over time, she began to see the benefits of removing and replenishing. Her stress levels decreased, and she was able to tackle her work with renewed focus and energy. She even found she had more time for personal matters, such as spending time with her family or pursuing her hobbies.

In the end, Tislum realized the power of time management and how simple changes can make a big difference in how she views her day. She continued to remove and replenish, making the most out of every hour, and her career success took off as a result.

There are plenty of time-wasting activities that people engage in without realizing it. Some examples include:

1. Mindlessly scrolling through social media feeds
2. Checking emails every few minutes
3. Multitasking on several activities at once
4. Attending unnecessary meetings or conference calls
5. Engaging in small talk or office gossip with coworkers

To replace these activities with more productive or fulfilling ones, people can try:

1. Taking a break to stretch, meditate, or practice deep breathing exercises
2. Prioritizing and scheduling email checking time slots during the day
3. Focusing on one task at a time and avoiding distractions
4. Creating agendas for meetings to ensure efficiency and purpose
5. Seeking out conversations with coworkers

that are informative or related to projects or goals, rather than gossip or idle chatter

One way to identify and prioritize important tasks is to create a to-do list and rank the tasks in order of importance or urgency. It's essential to be realistic about what can be accomplished in a day and to focus on completing one task before moving on to the next. It's also helpful to break down larger tasks into smaller, more manageable tasks to avoid feeling overwhelmed. Additionally, setting realistic deadlines and using time-blocking techniques can help individuals stay focused on one task at a time and avoid multitasking.

To ensure realism when creating a to-do list, individuals should consider their current workload and available time, as well as any potential obstacles or distractions that may arise. It's also important to prioritize tasks based on importance and deadline, and to be mindful of the time and effort required for each task. Seeking input from coworkers or supervisors can also ensure expectations are realistic and achievable. Additionally, regularly reviewing and revising the to-do list as needed can help individuals stay on track and avoid feeling overwhelmed.

To properly remove and replenish, it's important to prioritize self-care and take time for activities that promote relaxation and well-being. This might include things like exercise, meditation, spending time in nature, or engaging in hobbies and interests. It can also be helpful to identify and address the underlying causes of stress, such as work or relationship issues, and to seek support from friends, family, or a mental health professional if needed. Finally, practicing good time management and prioritization techniques, as discussed earlier, can help to reduce feelings of overwhelm and promote a more balanced and productive life.

CHAPTER THREE

ENGRAVE A SOLID MINDSET

There was a young man named Oluwafemi who struggled with negative self-talk and low confidence. He knew he wanted to be successful in life but couldn't seem to shake off the doubt holding him back.

One day, he came across a quote that read, "Your mindset is everything. It's the foundation for all success." Intrigued, he began to research the power of mindset, reading books on personal development and attending motivational seminars.

Slowly but surely, Oluwafemi began to engrave a solid mindset within himself. He practiced positive affirmations daily, reminding himself of his worth and capability. He surrounded himself with uplifting people, seeking out mentors who inspired and challenged him.

As time went on, Oluwafemi noticed a significant change in his life. Opportunities began to present themselves, and he found himself excelling in areas he once thought impossible. He had developed a strong sense of resilience and was able to handle setbacks with grace, bouncing back stronger than ever before.

Eventually, Oluwafemi realized that engraving a solid mindset was the key to his success. He knew that no matter what challenges may come his way, he had the inner strength and determination to overcome them. And with that knowledge, he continued to grow and thrive, living a life filled with purpose and fulfillment.

Some common ways people engrave a solid mindset within themselves include practicing positive affirmations, setting achievable goals, surrounding themselves with supportive and uplifting people, reading personal development books, attending motivational seminars, meditating or practicing mindfulness, and taking care of their physical health through exercise and healthy habits. It's important to find what works best for you and consistently practice these habits to build a strong and resilient mindset.

Yes, tracking progress and staying consistent with habits can definitely be challenging at times. That's why it's important to set realistic expectations and avoid being too hard on yourself if you slip up occasionally. To stay motivated throughout the process, it can be helpful to remind yourself of your reasons for wanting to build a strong mindset and remain resilient. You can also track your progress in a journal or app, celebrate small victories along the way, and enlist support from friends and family. Remember that building a strong mindset is a journey, and it's important to enjoy the process and trust in your ability to overcome obstacles.

Celebrating small victories can be a great way to stay motivated and build momentum. You can reward yourself with something like a small treat or a fun activity that you enjoy. It's also helpful to acknowledge the progress you've made and reflect on what you did well. This can help you stay focused on your goals and inspired to continue making progress. Remember, even small steps forward are worth celebrating!

Acknowledging progress and reflecting on accomplishments can be incredibly powerful for boosting motivation and momentum. When you take the time to recognize the progress you've made, it helps to build confidence and self-esteem, which can in turn fuel your motivation. Reflecting on accomplishments can also help you identify what's working well and what strategies are most effective for you, which can be incredibly helpful as you continue to work towards your goals. Additionally, reflecting on past successes can help you stay motivated during challenging times by reminding you of how capable you are and how far you've already come.

It's important to strike a balance between acknowledging your progress and staying focused on your goals. One way to do this is to set regular checkpoints or milestones along the way, so you can celebrate your progress while also keeping your eyes on the prize. Another helpful strategy is to avoid getting too caught up in your successes, and instead use them as fuel for continued growth and improvement. Remember, progress is rarely linear, and setbacks and challenges are inevitable. But if you stay focused and keep pushing forward, you'll be amazed at what you can achieve.

Staying motivated in the face of setbacks and challenges can be tough, but there are a few things you can do to help keep your motivation levels high. First, try to reframe your setbacks as opportunities for growth and learning. Every setback is a chance to identify areas where you can improve and develop new strategies for success. Second, stay focused on your why—remind yourself of the reasons why you set your goals in the first place and the benefits that achieving them will bring. Third, surround yourself with positive influences, like supportive friends and family or uplifting books and podcasts. And finally, take care of yourself—eat well, exercise regularly, and get enough rest and relaxation to keep a solid mindset and healthy body.

CHAPTER FOUR

ACTION AND ACCOUNTABILITY

Once, there was a young man named Khalil who had big dreams of starting his own business and being recognized globally as a talented basketball player. He had all the ideas and resources necessary to make it happen, but he struggled with taking action and holding himself accountable.

One day, Khalil decided enough was enough. He made a plan and set specific goals for himself to work towards each day. He also held himself accountable by committing to checking in with a coach every week to report on his progress.

At first, Khalil found it challenging to stick to his plan. He would often get distracted or lose focus, but he reminded himself of his why and the benefits that achieving his goals would bring. With each small accomplishment, he gained more confidence and momentum.

Over time, Khalil learned the importance of taking action and holding himself accountable. He realized that without these two elements, his dreams would remain nothing but dreams. By staying focused, persistent, and having the right support system, Khalil's business gradually grew and flourished. In the end, he became a successful entrepreneur and basketball player and an inspiration to many others who shared his dreams.

Khalil used several techniques to hold himself accountable for achieving his goals. First, he created a plan and set specific goals for himself to work towards each day. This helped him stay focused on what he needed to accomplish. Second, he committed to checking in with a coach every week to report on his progress. This provided him with an external source of accountability and support. Third, Khalil regularly reviewed his progress and adjusted his plan if necessary. This helped him stay on track and make the necessary adjustments to achieve his goals. Overall, Khalil's approach to accountability was systematic, balanced, and flexible.

Khalil's coach provided him with a sense of external accountability and support. By committing to check in with his coach every week, Khalil knew he had someone to report his progress to, keeping him motivated. His coach also provided him with valuable feedback and guidance, helping him stay on track and adjust his plan when needed. The coach acted as a sounding board for Khalil's ideas and helped him overcome any obstacles he encountered along the way. All of these factors contributed to Khalil's success in holding himself accountable and achieving his goals.

CHAPTER FIVE

NON-NEGOTIABLE

There once was a successful businessman named Antonio who created a set of non-negotiable principles that he lived and worked by. These principles dictated how he treated his colleagues, how he ran his business, and how he approached his personal life.

One day, a potential client approached Antonio with an offer that went against his non-negotiable principles. The client wanted him to cut corners and use unethical practices to secure a big contract. Despite the financial gain that could come from this deal, Antonio refused. He knew that compromising his values would ultimately lead to long-term negative consequences.

The potential client was upset with Antonio's refusal and tried to pressure him into changing his mind. But Antonio held firm and stood by his non-negotiable principles. Eventually, the client gave up and moved on to another business that was willing to compromise their values.

In the end, Antonio's commitment to his non-negotiable principles paid off. His business continued to thrive, and he gained a reputation for being a trustworthy and ethical leader. He knew that no amount of money or success was worth sacrificing his values for.

From then on, Antonio continued to live and work by his non-negotiable principles, and he inspired others to do the same. He proved that success is not just about achieving your goals but also about doing so in a way that aligns with your values and beliefs.

Antonio's non-negotiable principles included treating others with respect and honesty, being transparent in his business dealings, and always striving to do what was right, even if it meant missing out on short-term gains. These principles shaped his approach to business and life by guiding his decision-making and ensuring he stayed true to his values. He believed that success should not come at the expense of compromising one's integrity, and that doing the right thing ultimately leads to long-term success.

Antonio also believed in the importance of hard work, perseverance, and continuous learning. He knew that success is not handed on a silver platter, but rather, success comes because of your own efforts and determination. He also believed in giving back to his community and making a positive impact on the world around him, which he accomplished through charitable donations and volunteer work. These beliefs helped him stay focused on his goals and motivated to overcome obstacles along the way.

Yes, Antonio was very committed to spending time with his family and prioritized this time in his schedule. He believed that maintaining strong relationships with loved ones was essential for a fulfilling life, both personally and professionally. He made a point to schedule family time into his calendar and stick to it as much as possible, even if it meant saying no to other commitments. This allowed him to achieve a balance between work and family, which he believed was crucial for overall happiness and success.

Antonio valued both self-esteem and confidence and believed that these traits were essential for success in both business and life. He recognized that self-doubt and insecurity could hold him back, so he worked hard to build his self-esteem and confidence through various means such as positive self-talk and setting achievable goals. By maintaining a strong sense of self-worth and confidence, Antonio was able to take risks and pursue his goals with more vigor and determination.

Antonio's strong sense of self-esteem and confidence allowed him to take on new challenges and opportunities with ease. He was able to negotiate deals with confidence, build strong relationships with clients, and lead his team with conviction. In his personal life, he was able to pursue his passions and hobbies without fear of judgment or failure, which helped him develop a well-rounded and fulfilling life. Overall, Antonio's self-esteem and confidence were key factors in his success both professionally and personally.

Non-negotiables are things that you are not willing to compromise on or negotiate about. This could vary depending on the individual, but here are some examples:

1. Honesty and transparency in relationships
2. Safety and security in living or working environments
3. Personal values and beliefs
4. Boundaries around physical or emotional health
5. Fair treatment and respect in professional settings

6. Financial stability and responsibility
7. Commitments to family or loved ones

Effectively communicating your non-negotiables requires clarity, assertiveness, and respect for others. Here are some tips:

1. **Be clear and specific:** Clearly define what your non-negotiables are and explain why they are important to you.
2. **Use "I" statements:** Express your views and needs in a way that does not blame or criticize others.
3. **Be respectful:** Listen to the other person's perspective and try to find common ground where possible.
4. **Set boundaries:** Clearly communicate the consequences if someone violates your non-negotiables.
5. **Follow through:** Consistently enforce your non-negotiables and be willing to walk away from situations that do not meet your standards.

One approach could be to use "I" statements instead of "you" statements, the latter of which can come across as accusatory. It's important to also communicate your non-negotiables with a calm and respectful tone and to listen to the other person's perspective. You can also frame the conversation around finding common ground and understanding each other's needs. Lastly, it's important to set boundaries and consequences in a clear and assertive way, while still remaining respectful.

Navigating setting boundaries in a situation where the other person may not be receptive or respectful of your needs can be challenging, but it's important to stand your ground and stay firm in your beliefs. It may require setting consequences that are more severe or stepping back from the situation altogether. It's important to also take care of yourself and prioritize your own well-being. Seeking support from friends, family, or a therapist can be helpful in navigating these kinds of situations. Remember that you deserve to have your needs and boundaries respected, and you shouldn't be afraid to advocate for yourself.

Here are some specific strategies and tactics for setting and maintaining boundaries in challenging situations:

1. Use "I" statements to communicate your needs and expectations
2. Be assertive and firm in your boundaries while still remaining respectful
3. Consider setting consequences for violations of your boundaries and follow through with them
4. Take time to reflect on your boundaries and make sure they are reasonable and realistic
5. Practice self-care and prioritize your own well-being to avoid burnout
6. Seek support from others, whether it be friends, family, or a therapist
7. Don't be afraid to change your boundaries if they are not working for you
8. Keep an open mind and be willing to compromise while maintaining your non-negotiables

CHAPTER SIX

LIGHT INTO ENERGY

Once, there was a young entrepreneur named Raricus who was determined to start his own business. He had big dreams and ideas, but he lacked the resources and capital to make them a reality. However, Raricus was not one to be deterred by challenges. He knew that success requires hard work, dedication, and a willingness to take risks.

One evening, while sitting on the porch watching a thunderstorm roll in, Raricus was suddenly struck by an idea. He realized that lightning, which was so powerful and awe-inspiring, could be harnessed into energy. He decided to research the science behind lightning and began to develop a plan for how it could be turned into a sustainable source of energy.

Raricus worked tirelessly for months, pouring his heart and soul into the project. He faced many obstacles along the way and often felt like giving up. But he refused to let setbacks defeat him. He remained focused on the goal and persevered through the challenges.

Raricus faced many obstacles along the way, including skepticism and doubt from potential investors and clients and financial difficulties in funding his project. He also had to overcome legal and regulatory hurdles, as well as competition. Despite these challenges, he remained focused and determined, ultimately achieving his goals.

To overcome skepticism and doubt from potential investors and clients, Raricus relied on his technical expertise and research to demonstrate the feasibility of the project. He also engaged in extensive networking and outreach efforts to build relationships with key stakeholders and garner support for his vision. Additionally, he was able to secure some initial funding to get his project off the ground and prove its viability.

His company grew rapidly, and Raricus became a successful and respected businessman. He knew his success was due not only to the hard work and determination but also to the ability to think outside the box and take risks. Lightning Into Energy became a metaphor for his own journey towards success—a force to be reckoned with, powerful yet beautiful when harnessed properly.

Positive energy refers to a state of mind and emotions focused on optimism, joy, and gratitude. Mental energy refers to the cognitive abilities and mental focus needed to complete tasks and solve problems. Body energy refers to the physical strength and vitality required for movement and overall health. And mind energy refers to the power of intention and visualization in creating desired outcomes. All these types of energy can influence each other and contribute to overall well-being.

There are several techniques that can be helpful in increasing mind energy for better manifestation of goals. Some techniques include visualization, affirmations, meditation, goal setting, and positive self-talk. By focusing the mind on positive thoughts and beliefs and regularly visualizing success and desired outcomes, individuals can increase their mental energy and improve their ability to manifest their goals. Additionally, practicing gratitude and mindfulness can also help to maintain a positive and focused energy mindset.

CHAPTER SEVEN

GO TO THE CYCLE OF GROWTH

Tavian was a young entrepreneur who had a dream of starting his own business. He had a great idea and was very passionate about it, but he didn't know where to start.

Tavian decided to seek advice from a coach who had experience in entrepreneurship. The coach told him that success in business comes from trusting the process and being willing to repeat it over and over again.

Tavian took this advice to heart and began working on his business plan. He researched his market, identified potential customers, and started building his product. He faced many setbacks along the way, but he kept reminding himself to trust the process and keep moving forward.

When he launched his product, Tavian realized that his initial idea wasn't resonating with customers as much as he had hoped. Instead of giving up, he turned to his coach and sought feedback from his customers. He learned what they liked and didn't like about his product, and he used that information to improve it.

With each iteration, Tavian's product got better and better. He continued to trust the process and repeat it until he had a product that customers loved. He went through the cycle of growth several times, refining his product and refining his approach, until finally he had a successful business.

Tavian learned that success is not about having the perfect idea or the perfect plan. Success comes from trusting the process, being willing to repeat it, and being open to feedback and change.

Trusting the process involves having faith in your abilities and in the steps you have taken to achieve your goals. It also means being patient and willing to persevere despite setbacks or obstacles. To trust the process, it can help to break down your goals into smaller, more manageable steps and focus on each one at a time. It's also important to recognize that progress may be slow at times, but every step forward is a step closer to success.

Repeating the process involves going through the same cycle of growth, refining your product or approach, and taking feedback into account to improve it. It may involve testing and experimenting with different strategies, but this is always done with the goal of improving and learning from your experiences. Repeating the process also means being open to change and adapting as necessary based on new information or circumstances.

Balancing consistency with openness to change and adaptation involves finding a middle ground between rigidity and flexibility. You want to have clear goals and a firm foundation from which to work while also being open to new ideas and feedback that can help you improve your approach. It can be helpful to regularly assess your progress, taking stock of what's working and what isn't and being willing to make adjustments as needed. Ultimately, the key is to stay focused on your overall goals while remaining flexible and adaptable in how you approach them.

The cycle of growth describes the process that organizations go through as they grow and mature. It typically involves several stages, such as startup, growth, maturity, and decline. During the startup phase, the organization is focused on developing its product or service and building its customer base. As it grows, it may focus on expanding its market share, increasing efficiency, and optimizing its operations.

Effective management and adaptability are key to navigating each stage of the growth cycle successfully. There are several strategies that organizations can use to stay adaptable and resilient in the face of market saturation or increased competition.

Trusting the cycle of growth process can help individuals stay focused and motivated on their goals, rather than getting discouraged by setbacks or obstacles. By staying committed to a plan or approach, individuals can develop a sense of discipline and perseverance, which are both valuable traits for personal and professional growth.

Trusting the cycle of growth process can also help individuals develop resilience, as they learn to bounce back from setbacks and continue working towards their goals. Over time, this can lead to increased confidence and self-awareness, which can benefit individuals in all areas of their lives.

Trusting the cycle of growth process can lead to greater satisfaction and contentment in life by helping individuals focus on the journey rather than just the end result. When we trust the process, we learn to appreciate and enjoy the steps we take towards our goals, even if they are challenging or uncomfortable. This can help us develop a greater sense of gratitude for the present moment and all that we have accomplished so far. Additionally, when we achieve our goals through trusting the process, we can feel an incredible sense of satisfaction and fulfillment, knowing that we worked hard and overcame obstacles to get there. Overall, trusting the process and the cycle of growth can lead to a more joyful and fulfilling life.

JOURNAL QUESTIONS

1. What are your most cherished desires and goals in life?

_____

_____

_____

_____

_____

_____

_____

_____

2. How can you align your thoughts, emotions, and actions to manifest those desires?

_____

_____

_____

_____

_____

_____

_____

3. What beliefs or self-limiting patterns might be hindering your ability to manifest your goals?

_____

_____

_____

_____

_____

_____

_____

_____

4. What daily practices can you adopt to cultivate a positive and focused mindset for manifestation?

_____

_____

_____

_____

_____

_____

_____

_____

_____

5. How can you celebrate even the smallest manifestations in your life to build momentum and attract more abundance?

_____

_____

_____

_____

_____

_____

_____

_____

_____

_____

6. What steps can you take right now to start working towards your cherished desires and goals?

_____

_____

_____

_____

_____

_____

_____

_____

_____

_____

7. Have you considered seeking guidance or support from a mentor or coach to help you achieve your goals?

_____

_____

_____

_____

_____

_____

_____

_____

_____

_____

_____

_____

_____

_____

_____

_____

_____

_____

_____

_____

GREAN

LIGHT GO

TO 31 DAYS OF
MEDITATION JOURNAL

*Grean Light Go.... Make sure you write down your thoughts
and reflections in your journal after each meditation session.
Use this as a way to track your progress and reflect on your
transformation over the next 31 days.*

DAY ONE
BREATH MEDITATION

Breath meditation is an essential practice for keeping your anxiety in check and maintaining your composure, even in challenging situations. Here are some steps to get started:

1. Find a quiet, comfortable place where you won't be interrupted.
2. Sit or lie down in a comfortable position, close your eyes, and take a few deep breaths to relax.
3. Start by simply observing your breath without trying to change it.
4. Notice the sensation of the air flowing in and out of your nostrils. Pay attention to the rise and fall of your chest and belly.
5. If your mind starts to wander, gently bring your attention back to your breath.
6. You may choose to count your breaths or focus on a specific aspect of your breath, such as its rhythm, depth, or temperature.
7. Continue breathing naturally, staying present in the moment.
8. Once the meditation is complete, take a few moments to reflect on your experience and notice any changes in your thoughts, emotions, or physical sensations.

Remember to approach this practice with an open and relaxed attitude, allowing yourself to fully immerse in the present moment. With consistent practice, breathing meditation can help you reduce stress and anxiety, improve concentration and focus, and enhance overall well-being.

DAY TWO
SELF-LOVE MEDITATION

Self-love and self-acceptance are important practices for cultivating a positive relationship with yourself. Here are some steps to get started:

1. Practice self-compassion: Treat yourself with the same kindness, concern, and support that you would offer to someone you care about.
2. Challenge negative self-talk: Be aware of the negative thoughts or beliefs that you have about yourself and try replacing them with positive affirmations and self-talk.
3. Set realistic expectations: Give yourself permission to be imperfect and accept that mistakes and failures are a natural part of learning and growth.
4. Do activities that you enjoy: Engage in hobbies, interests, or activities that make you feel happy and fulfilled.
5. Nurture your body: Take care of your physical health by getting enough sleep, eating nutritious food, and exercising regularly.
6. Practice mindfulness: Cultivate awareness and acceptance of your thoughts, feelings, and sensations without judgment.

Remember that self-love and self-acceptance are lifelong journeys, and it's okay to struggle at times. With patience and consistency, you can develop a more compassionate and accepting relationship with yourself.

DAY THREE
GRATITUDE MEDITATION

Gratitude meditation involves focusing your attention on the things in your life for which you are grateful. Here are some steps to get started:

1. Begin by taking a few deep breaths to relax your body and mind.
2. Think of something you are grateful for, such as a person, a place, or a situation.
3. Focus your attention on this object of gratitude and try to hold it in your mind without judgment or distraction.
4. Notice any feelings of warmth, joy, or appreciation that arise as you focus on your gratitude.
5. If your mind wanders, gently bring your attention back to your object of gratitude.
6. Continue to focus on your gratitude for several minutes or more, depending on your comfort level.

Remember that gratitude meditation is a simple but powerful tool for cultivating a sense of abundance and happiness in your life. By practicing regularly, you can train your mind to focus on the good things in your life, even during difficult or challenging times.

DAY FOUR
FORGIVENESS MEDITATION

Forgiveness meditation is a powerful practice that can help you let go of resentment and anger towards others or yourself. Here are some steps to get started:

1. Take a few deep breaths to relax your body and mind.
2. Begin by focusing your attention on the person you need to forgive (even if it is yourself).
3. Repeat the following phrases silently or out loud: "I forgive you. I am sorry. I love you. Thank you."
4. As you repeat these phrases, try to visualize the person or situation that you are forgiving.
5. Notice any feelings of discomfort, pain, or resistance that arise, allowing yourself to feel them without judgment or criticism.
6. Repeat the phrases for several minutes or more, until you feel a sense of release and relief.

Remember that forgiveness meditation is not about condoning harmful behavior, but rather, it is about releasing the burden of resentment and anger that you carry. With time and practice, you can cultivate compassion and forgiveness towards yourself and others to experience greater peace and happiness in your life.

DAY FIVE
COMPASSION MEDITATION

Compassion meditation is a beautiful practice that can help you cultivate feelings of empathy and kindness towards yourself and others. Here are some steps to get started:

1. Take a few deep breaths and relax your body and mind.
2. Begin by focusing your attention on yourself or someone you want to send love and compassion to.
3. Repeat the following phrases silently or out loud: "May you be happy. May you be healthy. May you be safe. May you live with ease."
4. As you repeat these phrases, try to visualize the person or situation you want to send compassion towards.
5. Notice any feelings of warmth, peace, or joy that arise, allowing yourself to feel them fully.
6. Repeat the phrases for several minutes or more, until you feel a sense of connection and love.

Remember that compassion meditation is not about fixing or solving problems, but rather about opening your heart and cultivating feelings of care and kindness towards yourself and others. With time and practice, you can develop greater emotional resilience and empathy to experience more love and joy in your life.

DAY SIX
MINDFULNESS MEDITATION

Mindfulness meditation is a powerful practice that can help you cultivate greater awareness and be more present in the moment. Here are some steps to get started:

1. Take a few deep breaths and relax your body and mind.
2. Begin by focusing your attention on your breath, noticing the sensation of the air moving in and out of your body.
3. As thoughts or distractions arise, simply acknowledge them and gently bring your attention back to your breath.
4. Allow yourself to fully experience each moment as it unfolds, without judgment or resistance.
5. Notice any sensations, emotions, or thoughts that arise, and allow them to pass without getting caught up in them.
6. Practice for several minutes or more, until you feel a sense of calm and clarity.

Remember that mindfulness meditation is not about achieving a certain state of mind, but rather, it is about cultivating awareness and acceptance in the present moment. With time and practice, you can develop greater focus, resilience, and inner peace to experience a more fulfilling and meaningful life.

DAY SEVEN
GOAL VISUALIZATION MEDITATION

Goal visualization meditation is a powerful practice that can help you manifest your desires and achieve your goals. Here are some steps to get started:

1. Take a few deep breaths and relax your body and mind.
2. Close your eyes and begin to visualize yourself achieving your desired goal.
3. See yourself in vivid detail, actively engaging in the activities that will lead to your success.
4. Imagine how you will feel once you have achieved your goal—the sense of accomplishment, satisfaction, and fulfillment.
5. Use affirmations and positive self-talk to reinforce your belief in your ability to achieve your goal.
6. Stay focused on your vision, allowing yourself to experience the emotions associated with achieving your goal.

Remember that goal visualization meditation is not about wishful thinking or magical thinking. It's about creating a clear picture of what you want to achieve and visualizing yourself taking action towards it. With time and practice, you can develop greater clarity, motivation, and focus in order to bring your goals to fruition.

DAY EIGHT
REFLECTION MEDITATION

Reflection meditation is a practice that allows you to look inward and examine your thoughts and emotions without judgement. Here are some steps to get started:

1. Take a few deep breaths and relax your body and mind.
2. Close your eyes and recall a situation or feeling you want to reflect on.
3. Observe your thoughts and emotions as they come up, without judgment or the need to change them.
4. Allow yourself to fully experience the feelings associated with the situation or emotion.
5. Practice self-compassion and kindness towards yourself as you reflect on your experiences.
6. Use this time to gain insight and clarity about yourself and your emotions.

Remember that reflection meditation is not about fixing or changing anything. It's about gaining a deeper understanding of yourself and your experiences, and cultivating self-awareness and compassion. With time and practice, you can develop greater emotional intelligence and self-awareness to lead a more fulfilling and meaningful life.

DAY NINE
BODY SCAN MEDITATION

Body scan meditation is a practice that involves systematically scanning your body and bringing awareness to each part, from head to toe. The purpose of this meditation is to cultivate mindfulness and relaxation in the body. Here are some steps to get started:

1. Find a comfortable and quiet place to meditate.
2. Lie down or sit in a comfortable position and close your eyes.
3. Bring your attention to your breath and take a few deep breaths to relax your body.
4. Begin to mentally scan your body from the top of your head down to your toes, noting any sensations or discomfort as you go.
5. Try to keep your mind focused on the present moment, without getting caught up in thoughts or distractions.
6. If you notice any tension or discomfort in any part of your body, try to release it by using your breath and consciously relaxing the area.
7. After you have scanned your entire body, take a few deep breaths and bring your attention back to your breath.

Remember that body scan meditation is a great tool for reducing stress and anxiety as well as improving overall wellbeing. With time and practice, you can develop a greater sense of relaxation and awareness in your body to enjoy greater physical and emotional health.

_____

_____

_____

_____

_____

_____

_____

_____

_____

_____

_____

_____

_____

_____

_____

_____

_____

_____

_____

_____

_____

_____

_____

DAY TEN
INNER CHILD HEALING MEDITATION

Inner child healing meditation is a powerful practice that can help you heal emotional wounds and release negative patterns from childhood. Here are some steps to get started:

1. Sit comfortably and close your eyes.
2. Take a few deep breaths to ground yourself and bring your attention to the present moment.
3. Visualize yourself as a child and imagine you are holding your younger self in your arms.
4. Offer comforting and reassuring words to your inner child, such as "I am here for you" or "You are safe and loved."
5. Ask your inner child what they need or want from you and listen carefully to their response.
6. Express love, forgiveness, and compassion to your inner child, and allow yourself to release any negative feelings or emotions that arise.
7. When you feel ready, gently bring your awareness back to your body and take a few deep breaths.

Remember that inner child healing meditation can be a powerful tool for transforming negative patterns and cultivating greater self-love and compassion. With time and practice, you can develop a deeper connection to your inner child and experience greater peace and happiness in your life.

DAY ELEVEN
INNER WISDOM MEDITATION

Inner wisdom meditation is a practice that can help you tap into your intuition and connect with your inner guidance. Here are some steps to get started:

1. Take a few deep breaths to ground yourself and bring your attention to the present moment.
2. Visualize a bright light within you, symbolizing your inner wisdom.
3. Imagine this light growing brighter and expanding throughout your entire body and aura.
4. Invite your inner wisdom to speak to you and share any insights or guidance you need.
5. Be open to whatever messages or feelings come up, without judgement or resistance.
6. Thank your inner wisdom for any guidance received and trust that it will continue to guide you in the right direction.
7. When you feel ready, gently bring your awareness back to your body and take a few deep breaths.

Remember that inner wisdom meditation can be a powerful tool for accessing your own innate wisdom and finding clarity and direction in your life. With regular practice, you can cultivate a deeper connection to your intuition and make more aligned choices in all areas of your life.

DAY TWELVE
STRESS REDUCTION MEDITATION

Stress reduction meditation is a practice that can help you relax and let go of tension in your body and mind. Here are some steps to get started:

1. Sit comfortably with your back straight, either on a chair or on the floor with a cushion.
2. Close your eyes and take a few deep breaths to ground yourself and bring your attention to the present moment.
3. Focus on your breath, noticing how it feels as it enters and leaves your body.
4. As thoughts or distractions arise, gently acknowledge them then bring your attention back to your breath.
5. Visualize a peaceful scene, such as a calm beach or a quiet forest, and imagine yourself there, feeling relaxed and at ease.
6. Repeat a calming phrase or mantra, such as "peace" or "calm," to help focus your mind and anchor yourself in the present moment.
7. Allow yourself to feel any emotions or sensations that arise, without judgement or resistance.
8. When you feel ready, gently bring your awareness back to your body and take a few deep breaths.

Remember that stress reduction meditation can be a powerful tool for managing stress and promoting relaxation. With regular practice, you can develop greater resilience and peace of mind in the face of life's challenges.

DAY THIRTEEN
CHAKRA BALANCING MEDITATION

Chakra balancing meditation is a practice that can help you align and balance your body's energy centers, known as chakras. Here are some steps to get started:

1. Close your eyes and take a few deep breaths to ground yourself and bring your attention to the present moment.
2. Bring your attention to your root chakra, located at the base of your spine, and visualize a red light rotating clockwise.
3. Move your attention up to your sacral chakra, located below your navel, and visualize an orange light rotating clockwise.
4. Continue moving your attention up to your solar plexus chakra, located above your navel, and visualize a yellow light rotating clockwise.
5. Move on to your heart chakra, located in the center of your chest, and visualize a green light rotating clockwise.
6. Continue up to your throat chakra, located at your throat, and visualize a blue light rotating clockwise.
7. Move on to your third eye chakra, located between your eyebrows, and visualize an indigo light rotating clockwise.
8. Finally, bring your attention to your crown chakra, located at the top of your head, and visualize a violet light rotating clockwise.
9. Continue to focus on your breath as you balance and align each chakra.
10. When you feel ready, gently bring your awareness back to your body and take a few deep breaths.

Remember that chakra balancing meditation can help you align and balance your energy centers for greater physical, emotional, and spiritual well-being. With regular practice, you can cultivate a deeper connection to your inner wisdom and healing abilities.

DAY FOURTEEN
ABUNDANCE MINDSET MEDITATION

Abundance mindset meditation is a practice that aims to cultivate a mindset of abundance and prosperity. Here are some steps to get started:

1. Begin by finding a comfortable position, either sitting or lying down, and take a few deep breaths to calm your mind and body.
2. Visualize yourself standing in a beautiful, abundant garden filled with all kinds of fruits, vegetables, flowers, and trees. This garden represents the abundance that is available to you in all areas of your life.
3. Take a moment to give thanks for all the blessings in your life, both big and small, and embrace a sense of gratitude for all the abundance that surrounds you.
4. Focus on your heart center and imagine a golden light radiating outwards from your chest, filling your entire body with warmth and love.
5. Repeat the affirmation, "I am worthy of abundance and prosperity" several times, allowing the words to sink deeply into your subconscious mind.
6. Visualize yourself experiencing all the abundance that you desire, whether it's financial abundance, abundance in your relationships, or abundance in your health and well-being.
7. See yourself living a life of joy, fulfillment, and purpose, surrounded by the people and experiences that bring you happiness and satisfaction.
8. Take a few deep breaths and hold this vision of abundance in your mind, knowing that it is already manifesting in your life.
9. When you're ready, slowly open your eyes and return to

your day, feeling energized, inspired, and full of joyful anticipation for all the abundance that is coming your way.

DAY FIFTEEN
POSITIVE AFFIRMATION MEDITATION

Positive affirmation meditation is a practice that involves using positive statements or affirmations to rewire your thoughts and beliefs towards positivity, self-empowerment, and personal growth. Here are some steps to get started:

1. Take a few deep breaths, inhaling slowly and deeply through your nose, and exhaling through your mouth.
2. Close your eyes and focus on your breathing. Allow your thoughts to drift away as you become more relaxed.
3. Repeat the following affirmations to yourself silently or out loud:
   - "I am worthy of love and respect."
   - "I am capable of achieving my dreams and goals."
   - "I have the power to create a life filled with abundance and joy."
   - "I am grateful for all the blessings in my life."
4. Visualize these affirmations as if they are already true. See yourself surrounded by love, achieving your goals, experiencing abundance and joy, and feeling grateful for all that you have.
5. Continue to repeat these affirmations and visualize your desired outcomes for a few minutes.
6. When you're ready, slowly open your eyes and return to your day. Carry these positive affirmations with you throughout your day, noticing how they impact your thoughts and actions.

DAY SIXTEEN
HEALING FROM PAST TRAUMA MEDITATION

Healing from past trauma meditation is a practice that aims to support individuals in their journey of healing and recovery from past traumatic experiences. Here are some steps to get started:

1. Take a few deep breaths, inhaling slowly and deeply through your nose and exhaling through your mouth.
2. Close your eyes and focus on your breathing. Allow your thoughts to drift away as you become more relaxed.
3. Visualize yourself surrounded by a warm, loving, healing light.
4. Repeat the following affirmations to yourself silently or out loud:
   - "I release all pain and trauma from my past."
   - "I forgive those who have hurt me."
   - "I am free from the past and open to new opportunities and joy."
   - "I am worthy of love, happiness, and peace."
5. Visualize yourself letting go of all the pain and trauma from your past. See it being lifted away from you, allowing you to embrace the present moment with love and acceptance.
6. Take a moment to thank yourself for the strength and courage it takes to heal from past trauma.
7. When you're ready, slowly open your eyes and return to your day, feeling refreshed, healed, and ready to move forward with an open heart.

DAY SEVENTEEN
LETTING GO MEDITATION

Letting go meditation is a practice that focuses on releasing attachments, negative emotions, and thoughts that no longer serve you. Here are some steps to get started:

1. Take a few deep breaths, inhaling slowly and deeply through your nose and exhaling through your mouth.
2. Close your eyes and focus on your breathing. Allow your thoughts to drift away as you become more relaxed.
3. Visualize a balloon in front of you. Imagine that all of the negative emotions, thoughts, and memories that are weighing you down are inside the balloon.
4. See yourself releasing the balloon, watching it float away into the distance. As it disappears from view, feel a sense of release and freedom wash over you.
5. Repeat the following affirmations to yourself silently or out loud:
    - "I release all that no longer serves me."
    - "I am free from the past and open to new opportunities."
    - "I am worthy of love, happiness, and peace."
6. Visualize yourself letting go of all the things that are holding you back. See them being lifted away from you, allowing you to embrace the present moment with lightness and joy.
7. Take a moment to thank yourself for having the strength and courage to let go.
8. When you're ready, slowly open your eyes and return to your day, feeling refreshed, rejuvenated, and ready to move forward with a renewed sense of purpose.

DAY EIGHTEEN
CONNECTING WITH NATURE MEDITATION

Connecting with nature meditation is a practice that involves immersing oneself in the natural environment and using mindfulness techniques to deepen the connection and awareness of the natural world. Here are some steps to get started:

1. Find a peaceful, quiet place outdoors, preferably with greenery or natural surroundings.
2. Sit comfortably with your feet planted on the ground and your hands resting on your lap.
3. Take a few deep breaths, inhaling slowly and deeply through your nose and exhaling through your mouth.
4. Close your eyes and listen to the sounds around you. Hear the chirping of birds, rustling of leaves, and the gentle breeze.
5. Visualize yourself surrounded by nature—a lush forest, a serene ocean, or a beautiful garden.
6. Focus on the sensations of nature. Smell the fresh air, feel the warmth of the sun on your skin, and notice the colors and textures around you.
7. Connect with nature by using your senses. Touch the grass or soil beneath your feet, listen to the rustling of leaves, and breathe in the fresh air.
8. Repeat the following affirmations to yourself silently or out loud:
   - "I am one with nature."
   - "I am grateful for the beauty of the natural world."
   - "I am at peace with myself and the world around me."
9. Take a moment to enjoy the stillness and calmness of nature. Let it envelop you in its tranquility.
10. When you're ready, slowly open your eyes and return

to your day, feeling more grounded, centered, and connected to nature.

DAY NINETEEN
VISUALIZATION MANIFESTATION MEDITATION

Visualization manifestation meditation is a practice that combines the power of visualization and meditation to help manifest desired outcomes and goals in your life. Here are some steps to get started:

1. Take a few deep breaths, inhaling slowly and deeply through your nose and exhaling through your mouth.
2. Close your eyes and visualize the thing you want to manifest in your life, whether it's a new job, a relationship, or financial abundance.
3. Imagine yourself already having achieved this goal. See yourself in a new job, enjoying a fulfilling relationship, or living a life of abundance.
4. Use all your senses to bring your visualization to life. See yourself in vivid detail, feel the emotions associated with achieving your goal, hear any sounds that may be present, and taste or smell any relevant scents.
5. Repeat the following affirmations to yourself silently or out loud:
    • "I am worthy and capable of achieving my goals."
    • "I am open and receptive to the abundance of the universe."
    • "I trust the journey and have faith that everything is working out for my highest good."
6. Stay in this visualization for as long as you like, feeling the emotions associated with your manifestation coming to fruition.
7. When you're ready, slowly open your eyes and return to your day, carrying with you the feeling of already having achieved your goal.

DAY TWENTY
ENERGY CLEARING MEDITATION

Energy clearing meditation is a practice that involves the intentional release and purification of negative or stagnant energies from your mind, body, and environment. Here are some steps to get started:

1. Take a few deep breaths, inhaling slowly and deeply through your nose and exhaling through your mouth.
2. Close your eyes and imagine a bright light shining down from above, enveloping your entire body in its warmth and brightness.
3. See this light as a powerful force that is able to clear away any negative energy or blockages within your body and mind.
4. Focus on any areas of tension or stress within your body, and imagine the light penetrating those areas, clearing away any negative energy that may be lingering there.
5. Repeat the following affirmations to yourself silently or out loud:
   • "I release any negative energy that no longer serves me."
   • "I am open and receptive to positive energy and abundance."
   • "I am surrounded by love and light, and all is well."
6. Stay in this state of relaxation and visualization for as long as you like, feeling lighter and more grounded with each passing moment.
7. When you're ready, slowly open your eyes and return to your day, carrying with you the feeling of being fully energized and refreshed.

DAY TWENTY-ONE
SELF-CARE MEDITATION

Self-care meditation is a practice that focuses on nurturing and taking care of oneself on a deeper level to help you prioritize your wellbeing. Here are some steps to get started:

1. Take a few deep breaths, inhaling and exhaling slowly and deeply.
2. Close your eyes and bring your attention to the present moment.
3. Focus on your breath, feeling the air moving in and out of your body.
4. Begin a body scan, starting at your toes and moving upward until you reach the top of your head.
5. As you scan each part of your body, visualize it relaxing and releasing any tension or stress you may be carrying.
6. Repeat the following affirmations to yourself silently or out loud:
   - "I honor my body and prioritize my wellbeing."
   - "I am deserving of love, care, and nourishment."
   - "I give myself permission to rest and restore."
7. Stay in this state of relaxation and self-care for as long as you need, allowing yourself to feel fully supported and nurtured.
8. When you're ready, slowly open your eyes and return to your day, feeling grounded and rejuvenated.

DAY TWENTY-TWO
MINDFUL EATING MEDITATION

Mindful eating meditation is a practice that involves bringing full awareness and attention to the experience of eating to help you fully savor and enjoy your meals. Here are some steps to get started:

1. Look at your plate of food and take a moment to appreciate its colors, textures, and smells.
2. Take a deep breath and bring your attention to the present moment, focusing on the act of eating.
3. Take a small bite of food and savor it slowly and attentively.
4. Notice the flavors, textures, and sensations in your mouth as you chew.
5. Pay attention to your body's response to the food, noticing any feelings of pleasure, satisfaction, or discomfort.
6. Repeat this process with each bite, taking your time to fully engage with the experience of eating.
7. If your mind starts to wander, gently bring it back to the present moment and the act of eating.
8. When you have finished your meal, take a few deep breaths and thank yourself for taking the time to nourish your body and practice mindful eating.

Remember, the goal of mindful eating is not to restrict or judge yourself, but rather to fully engage with and enjoy the experience of eating.

DAY TWENTY-THREE
Inner Peace Meditation

Inner peace meditation is a practice that focuses on cultivating a state of tranquility, calmness, and inner harmony. Here are some steps to get started:

1. Take a deep breath and close your eyes, allowing yourself to fully relax and release any tension in your body.
2. Bring your attention to your breath, noticing the sensation of air moving in and out of your body with each inhale and exhale.
3. Visualize a peaceful and tranquil scene, such as a serene beach or a lush forest, and imagine yourself being fully immersed in this environment.
4. Allow any thoughts or feelings that arise to come and go without judgment, simply observing them from a place of detachment.
5. Focus on the present moment, letting go of any worries or concerns about the past or future.
6. Repeat a positive affirmation or mantra to yourself, such as "I am at peace" or "I am calm and centered."
7. Stay in this state of inner peace and relaxation for as long as you need, allowing yourself to fully soak up the tranquility and serenity of the moment.
8. When you're ready, slowly open your eyes and return to your day, feeling refreshed and rejuvenated.

Remember, inner peace is a state of mind and can be cultivated through regular practice and self-care.

DAY TWENTY-FOUR
GRATITUDE MEDITATION

Gratitude meditation is a practice that involves focusing on and cultivating feelings of gratitude for the present moment and the blessings in your life to help you appreciate the challenges in your life. Here are some steps to get started:

1. Take a deep breath and close your eyes, allowing yourself to fully relax and release any tension in your body.
2. Bring to mind a recent challenge or difficulty you've faced, whether it's something big or small.
3. Reflect on what this challenge has taught you or how it has helped you grow as a person.
4. Focus on the positive aspects of this experience, such as the opportunities it presented or the resilience and strength you discovered within yourself.
5. Express gratitude for this challenge and the lessons it has provided.
6. Repeat a positive affirmation or mantra to yourself, such as "I am grateful for the challenges that make me stronger" or "I am thankful for the growth that comes from adversity."
7. Stay in this state of gratitude and reflection for as long as you need, allowing yourself to fully appreciate the challenges in your life.
8. When you're ready, slowly open your eyes and return to your day, feeling empowered and grateful for the challenges that have shaped you into who you are today.

Remember, challenges are opportunities for growth, and practicing gratitude can help shift your perspective and transform difficult experiences into valuable learning opportunities.

DAY TWENTY-FIVE
CREATIVE VISUALIZATION MEDITATION

Creative visualization meditation is a practice that involves using the power of imagination and mental imagery to create desired outcomes and manifest goals. Here are some steps to get started:

1. Close your eyes and take a few deep breaths, allowing yourself to fully relax and let go of any tension or stress.
2. Begin to visualize a scene that brings you joy or peace - this could be a beach, a forest, a mountain top, or any other place that resonates with you.
3. Use all of your senses to bring this scene to life in your mind—feel the warmth of the sun on your skin, smell the fresh air or fragrant flowers, hear the sounds of birds or waves crashing against the shore.
4. Allow yourself to fully immerse in this scene, imagining yourself as an active participant rather than just an observer.
5. Create a specific intention or goal for this visualization; it could be to feel more relaxed, to find clarity on a decision, or to tap into your creativity.
6. As you continue to visualize, affirm your intention to yourself with positive and encouraging self-talk.
7. When you're ready, slowly bring yourself back to the present moment, taking deep breaths and allowing yourself to feel grounded and centered.

Remember, creative visualization can be a powerful tool for manifesting your goals and desires. By visualizing what you want to experience in your life, you can start to cultivate the energy and mindset needed to bring those experiences into reality.

DAY TWENTY-SIX
RELATIONSHIP HEALING MEDITATION

Relationship healing meditation is a practice that aims to heal and improve relationships, whether it be with oneself or with others. Here are some steps to get started:

1. Close your eyes and take a few deep breaths, allowing yourself to fully relax and let go of any tension or stress.
2. Visualize the person you want to heal your relationship with. See them in front of you, feeling their presence as if they were actually there.
3. Imagine a bright, healing light that surrounds both you and the other person. The light represents love, forgiveness, and understanding.
4. As you continue to visualize the light, allow yourself to release any negative thoughts or emotions about the relationship. Let go of any anger, hurt, or resentment that you may be holding onto.
5. Visualize a positive outcome for your relationship, whether it's improved communication, deeper connection, or renewed love and affection.
6. Affirm your intention to heal the relationship, repeating positive affirmations such as "I am willing to forgive and let go" or "Our relationship is filled with love and understanding."
7. When you're ready, slowly bring yourself back to the present moment, taking deep breaths and allowing yourself to feel grounded and centered.

Remember, healing a relationship takes time and effort, but visualization can be a powerful tool to help you shift your energy and mindset towards positive change.

DAY TWENTY-SEVEN
INTENTION SETTING MEDITATION

Intention setting meditation is a practice that involves setting clear and focused intentions for what you want to manifest or achieve in your life. Here are some steps to get started:

1. Close your eyes and take a few deep breaths, allowing yourself to fully relax and let go of any tension or stress.
2. Reflect on your intentions for the day, week, or month ahead. What do you want to manifest in your life? What goals do you want to achieve?
3. Visualize yourself already achieving your intentions. See yourself happy, fulfilled, and successful in all areas of your life.
4. Imagine a bright, positive energy radiating from within you, filling your entire being with light and abundance.
5. Repeat positive affirmations that align with your intentions, such as "I am capable of achieving my goals" or "I am deserving of success and happiness."
6. Take a moment to express gratitude for all the blessings in your life, and for the opportunities that will come your way.
7. When you're ready, slowly bring yourself back to the present moment, taking deep breaths and allowing yourself to feel grounded and centered.

Remember, setting intentions is one of the most powerful tools we have for creating positive change in our lives. Trust in the universe and believe in yourself, and you will manifest your dreams into reality.

DAY TWENTY-EIGHT
GROUNDING MEDITATION

Grounding meditation is a practice that focuses on establishing a connection with the present moment and the Earth, helping you feel centered, stable, and rooted in your body. Here are some steps to get started:

1. Take a few deep breaths and focus on your body, feeling the sensation of your breath entering and leaving your lungs.
2. Visualize roots growing out of the bottom of your feet, extending deep into the earth below you.
3. Imagine the earth's energy flowing up through these roots and into your body, filling you with strength, stability, and balance.
4. Focus on each part of your body, starting from your feet and moving upwards. Notice any tension or discomfort and allow it to release as you exhale.
5. Repeat positive affirmations to yourself, such as "I am grounded and centered" or "I am connected to the earth's energy and strength."
6. Take a moment to express gratitude for the support of the earth and all of nature.
7. When you're ready, slowly bring yourself back to the present moment, feeling refreshed, renewed, and grounded in your body and mind.

Grounding meditations can be incredibly beneficial for reducing stress and anxiety, increasing focus and clarity, and promoting overall well-being. Don't hesitate to try this meditation regularly to reap its full benefits!

DAY TWENTY-NINE
JOURNALING MEDITATION

Journaling meditation is a practice that combines the benefits of meditation and journaling. Here are some steps to get started:

1. Take a few deep breaths and allow yourself to relax in the present moment.
2. Set an intention for your journaling practice, such as exploring a specific emotion or problem, or simply reflecting on your day.
3. Begin writing in your journal, either free-form or in response to a specific prompt. Allow your thoughts and feelings to flow freely, without judgment or self-censorship.
4. As you write, notice any recurring themes or patterns. Pay attention to any insights or realizations that arise, and be open to new perspectives or solutions.
5. Take a moment to express gratitude for the opportunity to explore your inner thoughts and emotions through journaling.
6. When you're ready, slowly bring yourself back to the present moment, feeling grounded and centered in your body and mind.

Journaling meditations can be a powerful tool for self-discovery, emotional healing, and personal growth. Give it a try and see what insights you uncover!

DAY THIRTY
MANIFESTING ABUNDANCE MEDITATION

Manifesting abundance meditation is a practice that focuses on attracting abundance and prosperity into your life. Here are some steps to get started:

1. Close your eyes and take a few deep breaths, allowing yourself to relax and let go of any tension or stress.
2. Visualize yourself surrounded by abundance and prosperity in all areas of your life, whether it's financial, emotional, or spiritual.
3. Imagine yourself receiving everything you need and desire with ease and gratitude. See yourself enjoying the blessings of abundance in every moment.
4. Repeat positive affirmations to yourself, such as "I am abundant in all areas of my life" or "I attract abundance and prosperity effortlessly."
5. Feel the energy of abundance flowing through your body, filling you with joy, peace, and gratitude.
6. Take a moment to express gratitude for all the abundance and blessings in your life, both big and small.

Manifesting abundance meditations can be a powerful tool for attracting prosperity and success into your life. Give it a try and see what wonderful things come your way!

DAY THIRTY-ONE
LOVING KINDNESS MEDITATION

Loving kindness meditation is a practice that involves cultivating feelings of love, kindness, and compassion towards oneself and others. Here are some steps to get started:

1. Close your eyes and take a few deep breaths, allowing yourself to relax and let go of any tension or stress.
2. Begin by directing loving and compassionate thoughts towards yourself. Repeat the phrase, "May I be happy, may I be healthy, may I be safe, and may I live with ease."
3. Next, direct those same loving and compassionate thoughts towards a loved one. Picture them in your mind's eye and repeat the phrase, "May they be happy, may they be healthy, may they be safe, and may they live with ease."
4. Now, direct those same loving and compassionate thoughts towards someone you feel neutral towards. It could be a stranger, a colleague, or someone you don't know well. Repeat the phrase, "May they be happy, may they be healthy, may they be safe, and may they live with ease."
5. Lastly, direct those same loving and compassionate thoughts towards someone who challenges you or towards someone you have negative feelings about. Repeat the phrase, "May they be happy, may they be healthy, may they be safe, and may they live with ease."
6. Take a moment to visualize all of these individuals surrounded by love and compassion. Feel the positive energy flowing through your body and out into the world.

Loving kindness meditations can be a powerful tool for cultivating compassion, empathy, and positivity in your life. Give it a try and see how it can transform your relationships and outlook on life!

_____

_____

_____

_____

_____

_____

_____

_____

_____

_____

_____

_____

_____

_____

_____

_____

_____

_____

_____

_____

_____

_____

_____

About the Author

Tangela Huggins is an African American author, entrepreneur, TV personality, transformational coach, and motivational speaker known for empowering and motivating people through writing and speaking about her childhood trauma. Growing up, Tangela faced a tumultuous childhood, filled with abuse and neglect. Tangela has faced many high points as well as low points in her life, all of which has shaped her into the fierce black African American woman she is today. She has successfully turned challenging moments into transformational life lessons for not only herself but also for those she inspires.

Tangela overcame an unhealthy amount of adversity and tragedy growing up. These traumatic events in her childhood helped to develop her resilience and passion to help and free others. In her early adulthood as a single mom of three, Tangela moved out of state and attended Mercer University, where she studied accounting. However, after not receiving the gratification she desired while working in corporate America, she became a successful serial entrepreneur.

Tangela has a passion and calling to help people in need, mentally, physically, and financially. Her unique story shows why she is important and why she deserves a platform. She created a technique called "Grean Light Go" for self, career, business, and health development. Tangela uses her platform to empower and encourage people in need, as she guides them on a transformational path through motivation and transformation.

www.ingramcontent.com/pod-product-compliance
Lightning Source LLC
Chambersburg PA
CBHW032004060426
42449CB00031B/399